POEM

A Mashup

M. D. Usher

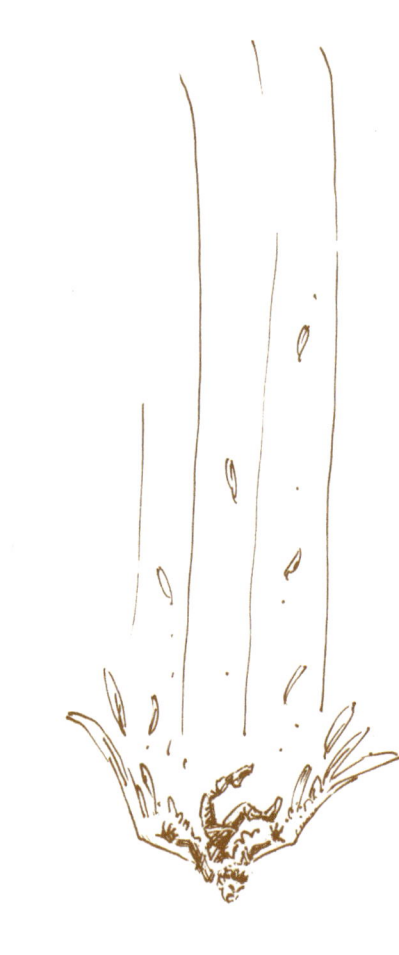

T. Motley

Poem
A Mashup

text by M. D. Usher

illustrated by T. Motley

Fomite
Burlington, VT

Text © M. D. Usher 2022
Illustrations © T. Motley 2022
All rights reserved. No part of this book may be reproduced in any form or by any means without the prior written consent of the publisher, except in the case of brief quotations used in reviews and certain other noncommercial uses permitted by copyright law.

ISBN-13: 978-1-953236-51-7
Library of Congress Control Number: 2021947950
Fomite
58 Peru Street
Burlington, VT 05401
www.fomitepress.com

01-08-2022

Proem to *POEM*

This is an illustrated book for readers aged nine to ninety. (PG-13 for age nine.) It is, so far as I can tell, *sui generis*, that is to say (if I may say so), wholly unique. The text of *POEM* is what is known as a cento, or "patchwork": it stitches together lines and phrases of famous existing poems to form an entirely new, and itself poetic, whole. The result is something like a pastiche introduction to the conventions of poetry—its sounds, images, aims, and rhythms—in which the words of the text illustrate the aspect of poetry that is being presented. In this respect, the book might be described as an "Ars Poetica" (Horace's old hashtag) or "Essay on Criticism" (Alexander Pope's) for the aspiring wordsmith. But the aesthetic of *POEM* is much more modern than all that hallowed literary tradition implies. One might even say it is postmodern, akin to a popular musical form—digital sampling, remixing, and so-called "mashup"—in which unexpected combinations of familiar lines and phrases yield new rhythms and rhymes and give the poetry of the verbatim original a new dimension. I realize full well that this makes me something closer to a DJ than an author. But that's OK. DJs bring life to the party.

In creating the text, I have drawn from a wide swatch of representative poems that are well enough known to be at least vaguely familiar to most ears. Poets featured range from Shakespeare, Milton, and Blake, to Dickinson, cummings, Eliot, and others. (In some places, I have slightly adapted the borrowed lines and phrases to make them mesh in their new setting.) It is hoped that *POEM's* "remix" of well-known snippets from canonical poets will become a soundtrack for subway commutes, a mantra for meditators, and a bedtime story for Bonzo.

From the outset I envisaged this project as a book version for poetry of what the film *Fantasia* is to classical music. In *Fantasia* (1940), animation brings the music of Bach, Stravinsky, and other composers literally to life, creating a context and atmosphere for the viewer to interpret the sounds. T. Motley's phantasmagoric illustrations, in which text is incorporated ingeniously into image, does exactly this. It is as if Word became Flesh and stood in front of a funhouse mirror. Some of the poetic images in *POEM* are whimsical. Others are serious, psychedelic, and emotionally profound. All, however, are solidly within the sphere of anyone's experience, young or old, and certainly within the scope of readers' imaginations. Nearly every image contains a recognizable visual allusion of some kind, so the pictures reward close inspection.

Poets featured in this fabric receive brief biographical treatment at the back of the book ("A Rogues' Gallery of Poets Featured in

POEM"). These miniature bios do double duty as a critical assessment of/statement about each poet's work and provide the source and context for all the lines and phrases embroidered into the main text. A short bibliography of accessible works on poetry would make a book like this a useful resource, so I have included one.

Poetry today is mostly read only by other poets, especially by would-be poets, and within even that small circle most of it is read only by the poet's family and friends (and perhaps also by the more cunning of her enemies). *POEM* seeks to enlarge the huddle, to invite young readers of all ages and of every kind to join in the fun. Freud thought there was an intimate link—a kinship of genius, one might say—between primitives and children. Both believe in the Omnipotence of Thoughts, Freud's term for a worldview in which actual things are less important than ideas of things. From this source springs both the spell-casting magician and the cave painters of Lascaux. Poetry is, at its core, a similar expression of such wish fulfillment and narcissism, qualities that primitives and children share with modern neurotics. If you want to see and experience the childhood of the world, I say: Look to the poets.

is an ancient word

ΠΟΙΗΜΑ

born from a verb that means

and poets MAKE

whatever they PLEASE

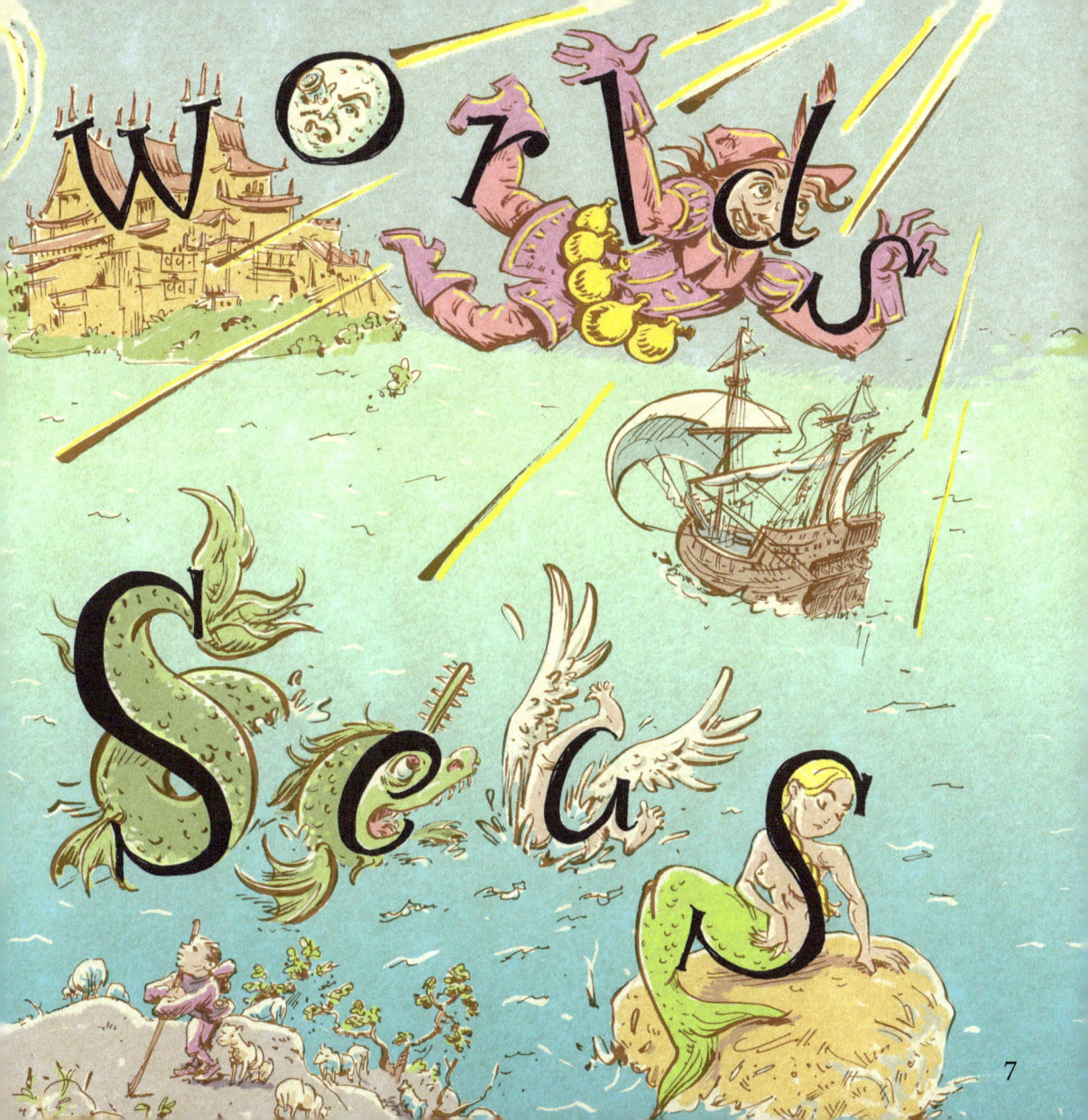

before annihilating all that's made

There can be a poem in a single word—

a Barbaric YAWP,

or Om, ॐ Shalom, Salaam, Amen.

into syllables and sounds, like...

Hickety-pickety, goosey gander,

Heigh diddle diddle, and dickory dock, or...

a poem, like a beam of light,

or it can bloody the sun with dizzying leaves

Some poems ask you questions—

And then confide in you just what they think:

> How dreary — to be — Somebody!

> How public — like a Frog —

to tell one's
name —
the
livelong
June —

B

24

a poem
can be
s l o w
and

or a poem can be as quick

onetwothreefourfive

to say

pigeonsjustlikethat!

some poems come in on little catfeet

Some wander lonely as a cloud

But sometimes poets can only sing with a whimper, not a bang.

Poets sing of Heroes too,
All glorious and great,

But poets also serve Who only stand and wait.

A poem says

"I Love You: Let me count the ways"

It can say **I HATE** things too, or with *Peaceful words* UPRAISE

ODI ET AMO

Poems take you on a journey...

Let us go then, you and I,
when the evening is
spread out against
the sky,

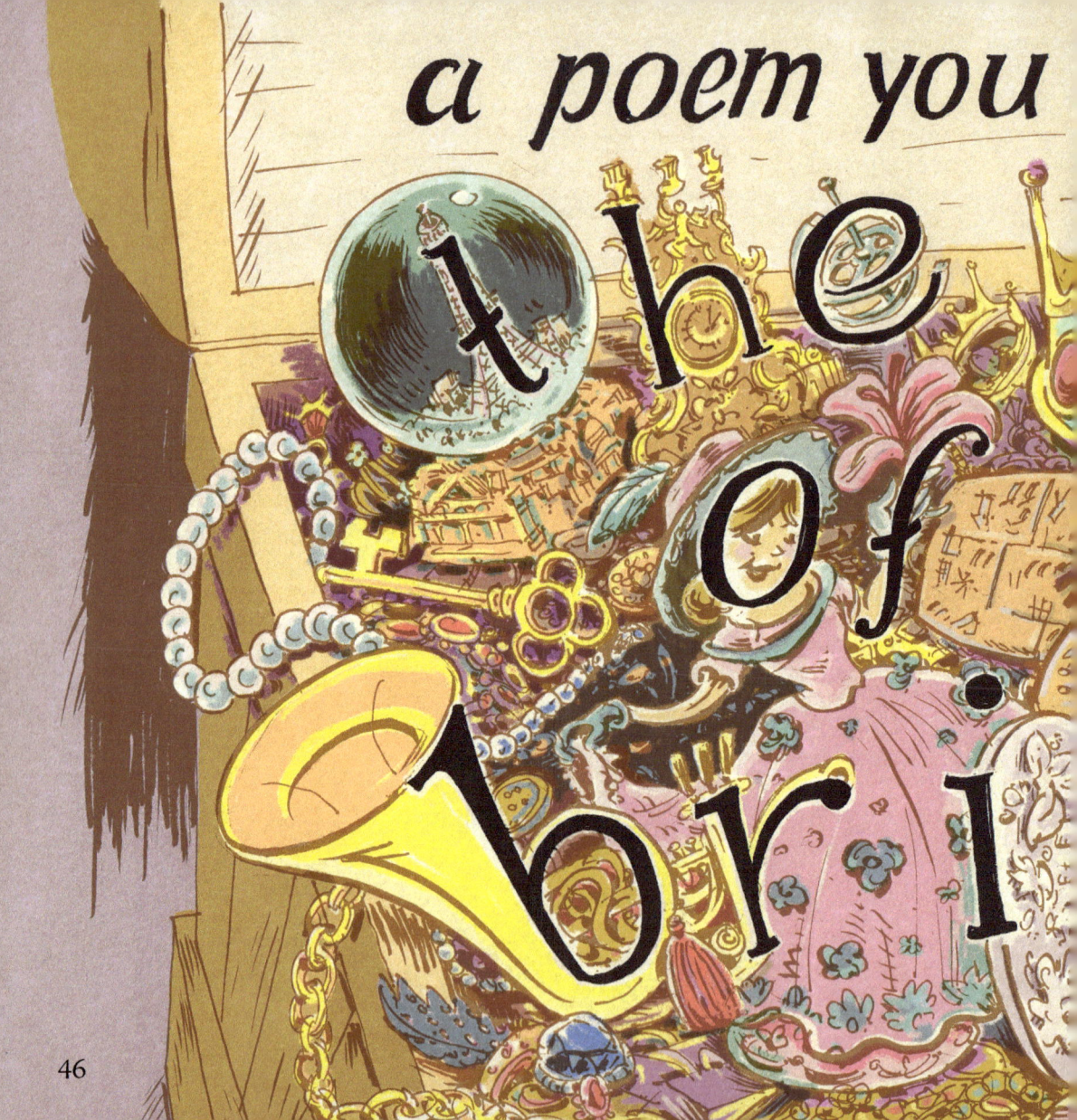

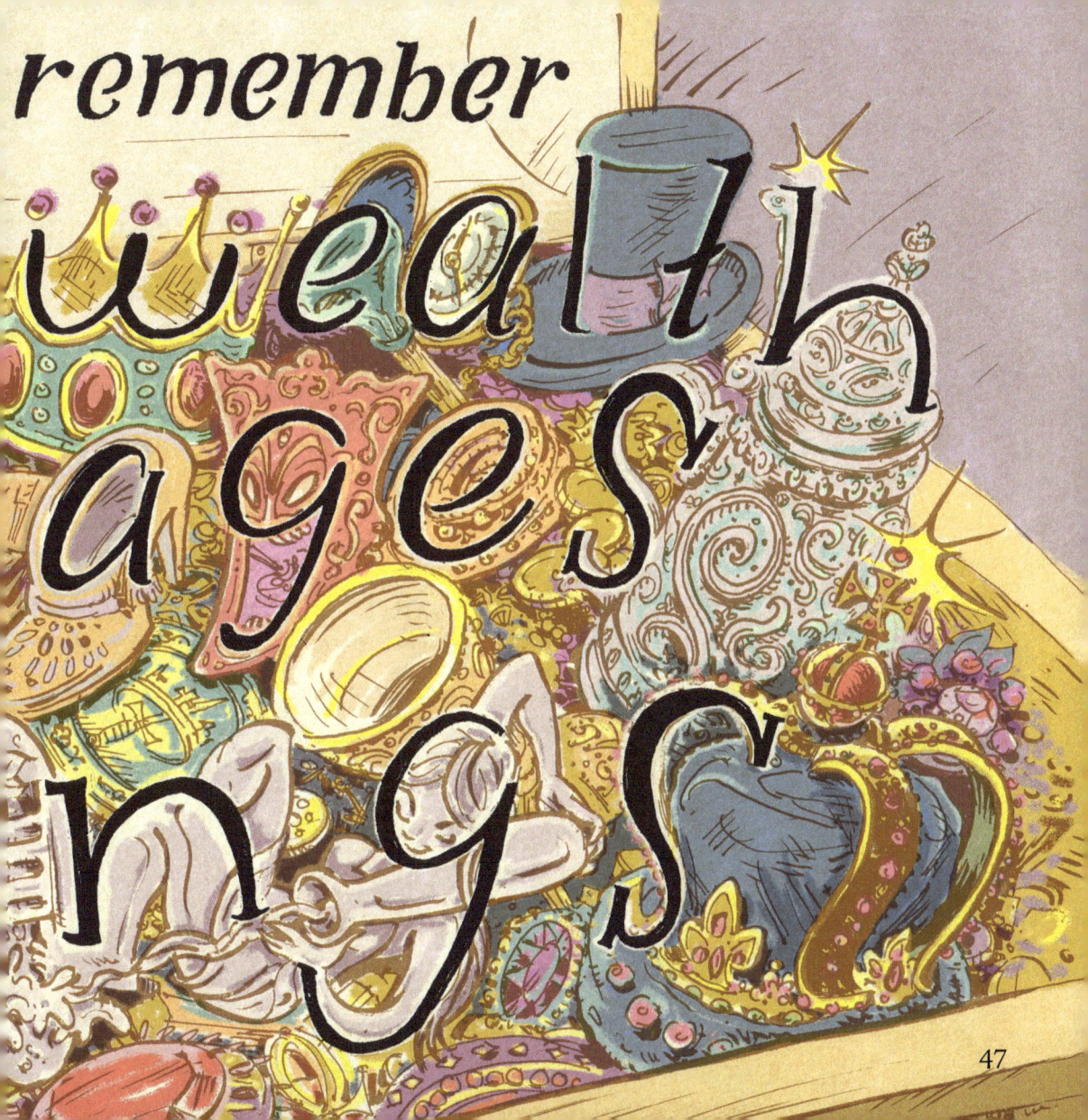

Such Riche$ that you'll scorn to change your lowly state with Kings

Finis

Rogues Gallery of Poets Featured in *POEM*, in Order of Appearance . . .

Ezra Pound (1885-1972)

There is only a faint whiff of Ezra Pound in this book. That might be plenty enough already for some readers who find he still reeks from the stench of Mussolini's Italy, where Pound, an American from Idaho, lived most of his adult life. Somehow Pound got himself mixed up with broadcasts on Fascist radio during the Second World War. This branded him a traitor, then landed him in a cage when the Allies took control of Italy. From there all roads led to St. Elizabeth's asylum for the insane in Washington, D.C., where Pound spent the rest of all but a few of his last years. All the while, though, he wrote poems. Good poems. His early poems are especially good. When not writing poems, Pound wrote prose. A lot of it. More than most poets tend to write. Books like **Guide to Kulchur** (1938) and *ABC of Reading* (1934) are opinionated works of criticism and theorizing. When Pound wanted to shout at you to get your attention, he used

UPPER CASE, which we mimic in the opening pages ("And poets MAKE whatever they PLEASE..."). But I'll let Pound shout at you himself, from *ABC of Reading*, a passage that contains his trademark aesthetic in a nutshell: "Literature is news that STAYS news."

Andrew Marvell (1621-1678)
Andrew Marvell lived in those heady days when promising young scholars went up to Oxford at age 12, having by then already achieved mastery in ancient Greek and Latin at grammar school. (*O tempora! O mores!*) Learned and ever playful, the mature Marvell, by then Latin Secretary to Oliver Cromwell and a member of Parliament, composed a Latin version of his magisterial poem "The Garden," from which we've excerpted some phrases on pages 6-9. The Latin version is called, predictably, "Hortus."
In the English original the full stanza in which our excerpt appears (stanza no. VI) goes like this:

> Meanwhile the Mind, from pleasure less,
> Withdraws into its happiness:
> The Mind, that Ocean where each kind
> Does straight its own resemblance find;

> Yet it creates, transcending these,
> Far other Worlds, and other Seas;
> Annihilating all that's made
> To a green Thought in a green Shade.

Before getting to the Latin, the Ocean reference, I suspect, needs explaining. In Marvell's day, theological speculation held that Creation must be symmetrical to be perfect and that every creature on earth would therefore have its counterpart in the sea. Marvell cheekily invokes this zany theory to suggest the Mind has the power, by ideation, not only to replicate what exists in Nature, but to go quite beyond it (i.e., "far other Worlds and other Seas"). In Marvell's Latin version of "The Garden" we find the green plants and green shade (*Plantae virides, & concolor Umbra*) into which the poet wishes to withdraw from the bustle and boredom of everyday life, but no Mind. That's interesting. In describing the garden as a pleasure-dome for retreat, Marvell is mostly imitating his Latin sources (the poetry of Horace in particular). In extolling Mind, however, he shows himself to be a poet of his own time. Marvell was one of a group of poets (including John Donne, who will make his own appearance later) that Samuel Dr. Johnson later called (pejoratively) "Metaphysical." The Metaphysical Poets had a knack for seeing in their mind's eye uncanny resemblances between quite dissimilar things, creating thereby a type of super-metaphor called a conceit. The doctrine that the Mind has the power to create then obliterate at will, in one fell swoop, and/or to transport itself from the dross of daily living to a garden of delight, takes metaphor to a whole new plane. Who would not want to be a poet if that were the case? That's tantamount to Divinity itself.

Walt Whitman (1819-1892)

If there were a Mount Rushmore for poets, Walt Whitman would be sculpted on it. So, too, for that matter, Carl Sandburg, Robert Frost, and Emily Dickinson (all of whom also make cameo appearances in *POEM*). If we take the analogy seriously, as poets tend to do, I suppose that would make Emily Dickinson the first female President of the United States. Good result! Be that, however, as it may, Whitman's iconic beard, straw hat, capacious intellect, and humungous poetic heart easily qualifies him to be immortalized as a founding father of American poetry. The phrase "barbaric yawp" on page 10 appears in Whitman's "Song of Myself," the signature poem in his *magnum opus*, that Bible of American experience and imagination, *Leaves of Grass*. "I too am not a bit tamed—I too am untranslatable," Whitman sings. "I sound my barbaric yawp over the roofs of the world." One would ordinarily give the date a cited book was published in parentheses here, but the thing about Whitman, of which every would-be poet should stand up and take notice, is how inclined he was to enlarge and revise his work: New editions of *Leaves of Grass* appeared in 1856, 1860, 1867, 1871–72, and 1881 after the book's first printing in 1855. You could say the guy stuck with things.

Mother Goose (???)

Based on what we can reliably discern, Mother Goose was a man. In 1697 Charles Perrault (1628-1703) published *Contes de ma Mère l'Oye* ("Tales of My Mother Goose"), a collection that has given us some perennial folkloric favorites like "Little Red Riding Hood," "Cinderella," and "Sleeping Beauty." Once Perrault's work had been translated into English, the name Mother Goose also came to be associated with English nursery rhymes, snippets of which appear on pages 14-15. Some have speculated that the name "Mother Goose" originates with Bertha of Burgundy (964-1010), second wife of King Robert II of France, who for some reason had attracted the moniker "Goose-footed Bertha" (*Berthe pied d'oie*), but was also known as "Bertha the Spinner" (*Berthe la fileuse*) for her apparent talent in spinning yarns for children. Whatever the truth or non-truth of that, the sing-song, sing-along quality of Mother Goose rhymes, combined with their mysterious, sometimes dark, socio-historical references, make them wholly captivating for young and old alike. They are, one might say, the quintessence of poetry in that they are rooted in sound and orality. Nursery rhymes reach something of a high art form in Edward Lear (1812-1888), whose nonsense poems are the verbal equivalent of absurdist art well before Max Ernst or Marcel Duchamp were opening their lunchboxes at school. It is hard not to think that Lear had old Mother Goose's

"Hey diddle-diddle" in mind when he penned the last lines of his exquisite lay "The Owl and the Pussycat," from 1871:

> They dined on mince and slices of quince
>   Which they ate with a runcible spoon;
> And hand in hand, on the edge of the sand
>   They danced by the light of the moon.
>   The moon,
>   The moon,
> They danced by the light of the moon.

Lewis Carroll (1832-1898)

Speaking of nonsense and 1871, that was the year and the genre in which Charles Dodgson, aka Lewis Carroll, composed "Jabberwocky," a poem embedded in *Through the Looking-Glass, and What Alice Found There.* Dodgson's "Jabberwocky" has blessed the world with the eerie neologisms that appear on pages 16-17. The poet himself was an equally rare bird—an accomplished mathematician by profession, a photographer by avocation, and a philosopher-cum-Anglican deacon and children's author in his spare time. Dodgson was so rare, in fact, that his avatar in the prequel to *Through the Looking Glass*—*Alice's Adventures in Wonderland* (1865)—is the Dodo. It has been suggested that Dodgson, a known stutterer, insinuated himself as the Dodo because whenever he introduced himself his name inevitably came out as "Do-do-dodgson." The story is probably apocryphal, but it suits such a sensitive, resourceful soul to create hilarity out of a handicap. This is the man, after all, who cast a seven-year old girl as vanquisher of the monstrous chaos, caprice, and cruelty of Wonderland. The Victorians got many things wrong, but what they did not lack in an age without television and the internet is imagination. What really brings Dodgson's Alice books to life for me are the illustrations by John Tenniel (1820-1914). These have become as iconic and definitive as the text itself, though T. Motley's Jabberwock, I must aver, gives Tenniel's a run for its money.

Dylan Thomas (1914-1953)

"Do not go gently into that good night" is how Dylan Thomas characterized his philosophy of life and death. "Old age should burn and rave at close of day," he muses defiantly. "Rage, rage against the dying of the light." Thomas himself did plenty rage, and burned his own candle at both ends. Indeed, he burned it to the ground at age thirty-nine, his life extinguished by a toxic mixture of alcohol, a festering bronchial affliction, and a well-meaning, but fatal ministration of phenobarbital by a friend. The result? As he says elsewhere in the poem excerpted on pages 18-19: "Where no wax is, the candle shows its hairs." The poem in question, titled "Light Breaks Where No Sun Shines," was published in 1934, when Thomas was aged but twenty. It follows a tight metrical pattern over successive stanzas, using bizarre imagery and archaic phraseology and word order to achieve its effects. Formalism and archaism in fact typify all of Thomas's poems. Far from being a straightjacket that confines poetic expression, form and meter provide a structure in which to realize poetic opportunities. Many of Thomas's poems sound to me like talking points for a bender, followed by a hangover. He seems to cling to form as if it were the sleeve of a fellow barfly. That is, he uses it to think things through, and to steady himself. This is not a criticism. It is a compliment. Thomas understood, perhaps better than most, that we are all "broken ghosts with glow-worms in [our] heads." Yet we are at the same time, as he puts it in the next line of that same stanza, "things of light," *Lux in Tenebris*. The poems we write, or aspire to write, like beams of light, can break where no sun shines.

e. e. cummings (1894-1962)

By his own account, Edward Estlin ("e. e.") Cummings enjoyed a happy childhood surrounded by a loving family. That is already unusual for an artist. But his body of work is also unusual, perhaps because his creativity was so supported and encouraged when he was young. (He began writing a poem a day from age eight.) Cummings' poetry is notable, visually, for its lack of capitalization, experimental spacing and punctuation, and what ancient Greek critics called *hyperbaton* (disjointed word order) and *katachresis* (misuse of parts of speech). But such bling is not his work's most salient feature. What stands out is an unapologetic, child-like lyricism. In an age of irony and cynicism (that would be every age) cummings wrote poems like this:

> i thank You God for most this amazing
> day:for the leaping greenly spirits of trees
> and a blue true dream of sky;and for everything
> which is natural which is infinite which is yes

In the full poem excerpted on pages 20-21 ("what if a much of a which of a wind") cummings pulls out all the stops and blasts us with his full organ of poetic technique. The result is considerably bleaker than "i thank You God." "What if a much of a which of a wind" is an apocalyptic vision of cataclysms, both natural and man-made, wherein "the most who die, the more we live." Whatever that means exactly, it seems a parable for our times.

Cummings appears again on page 28-29, a line lifted from a paean to many a childhood hero—William "Buffalo Bill" Cody, frontier cowboy, gold digger, Civil War soldier, and circus showman. Buffalo Bill fans his six-gun to knock off pigeons in such rapid succession that there are no spaces between the words. (To assuage sensitive readers concerned about ornithological welfare, we are probably being asked to imagine clay pigeons, pulled for target practice.) Cummings croons approvingly with boyish admiration: "Jesus / he was a handsome man." But that's a sentiment after-the- fact, since, as the poet says in his opening salvo, "Buffalo Bill's defunct." The concluding apostrophe of this short, pistol-shaped tribute to Buffalo Bill restates that bald pronouncement, suggesting that even buoyant lyricism must sometimes have its darker side: "how do you like your blue-eyed boy / Mister Death"?

Emily Dickinson (1830-1886)

Emily Dickinson's poems are littered with em dashes. This idiosyncratic feature of her work is also the story of her life. She would deliver a letter to a friend, ring the bell—then dash off before her friend came to the door. She'd happily play the piano for you—but only if you sat in the next room. Her favorite day of the week was Sunday. That was when her family went to church and left her alone—at home. The rationale for her reclusion sounds like an article of faith: *The Soul selects her own Society—*, she writes, *Then—shuts the Door—/ To her divine Majority—/ Present no more—*. Dickinson's terse poetic lines reflect an outwardly repressed personality. Yet, as if by way of compensation, they gleam with an introverted exuberance. Her poems also instantiate the ideal, captured in the German verb *dichten*, that poetry's job is "to condense" one's thoughts and emotions. The lines excerpted on pages 22-23 reflect this aesthetic, and underscore another facet of Dickinson's *oeuvre*—namely, how playfully unconcerned she was with worldly pursuits or success. "I am Nobody"? Dickinson is the *patron saint* of Nobodies. She wrote poems for her own pleasure and fulfillment. Perhaps also for her sanity. Apart from a few pieces published anonymously in local newspapers, everything she ever wrote—some 1,800 poems—was discovered stuffed in a drawer by her sister Lavinia only after her death. That cache is a poetic word-hoard so original and unique that it defies comparison with predecessors. Her originality and the posthumous, unsought attention her poems now enjoy offer hope and solace to all poetic introverts who revel in the profundity of the mundane and try to put their thoughts and feelings on paper.

Thomas Gray (1716-1771)

Here are some numbers: 1) Gray published only thirteen poems in his lifetime; 2) Of twelve children born to his mother, Thomas was the only one to survive infancy; 3) His father was an abusive madman. This last, admittedly, is not a number. But it is a significant piece of data about Gray's development. In any event, the numbers all add up to make it not at all surprising that an elegy—a poem of mourning and melancholic reflection—was likely to be among his baker's dozen. Gray's "Elegy Written in a Country Churchyard" is actually considered among the finest poems in the English language. We get a slew of now commonplace phrases from it; e.g., "far from the madding crowd," "unlettered muse," and "kindred spirit." The lines about the ploughman on page 27 appear in the opening stanza and exemplify a subtle use of *onomatopoeia*. (You can almost hear how slowly the tired ploughman is walking home after a long day's work.)

> The curfew tolls the knell of parting day,
> > The lowing herd wind slowly o'er the lea,
> The ploughman homeward plods his weary way,
> > And leaves the world to darkness and to me.

In spite of his rough start in life, young Thomas nonetheless did well for himself. His single-parent mother managed to send him to Eton, then to Cambridge, where he later became an endowed professor. Gray was cozy with the leading luminaries of his day, but he was by nature a retiring man, happiest to bide his time playing Scarlatti on the harpsichord or reading Pindaric Odes in his study.

Carl Sandburg (1878-1967)

Carl Sandburg might be the most interesting person featured in this book. He was so much more than a poet. Born in a three-room shack in Illinois, Sandburg left school at thirteen and worked dozens of odd jobs as, e.g., milkman, bricklayer, hotel porter, farm laborer, and coal-heaver. He was stationed in Puerto Rico during the Spanish-American War. In between there were aborted stints at Lombard College and West Point before his entrée into the world of letters as a newspaperman. Sandburg was self-made and self-taught, which makes the three Pulitzer Prizes he won particularly impressive (two for poetry; one for history). He even won a Grammy. Indeed, that is another remarkable thing about Sandburg—he was a songster. He would often accompany himself on guitar at lectures and poetry recitals. He compiled a popular and influential anthology of American folk music, *The American Songbag*, in 1927. As a musical artist and collector Sandburg anticipated by decades the folk revivals of the 1940s and 60s. He was Alan Lomax, Leadbelly, and Woody Guthrie rolled into one.

A phrase from Sandburg's poem "Fog" appears on page 30. "The fog," Sandburg intones in this haiku-like poem, "comes on little cat feet.

> It sits looking
> over harbor and city on
> silent haunches and
> then moves on.

"Fog" appeared in the volume *Chicago Poems* in 1916. When Sandburg famously describes its titular city as

> Hog Butcher for the World,
>   Tool Maker, Stacker of Wheat,
>   Player with Railroads and the Nation's Freight Handler;
>   Stormy, husky, brawling,
>   City of the Big Shoulders

it is hard not to think that the poet's Windy City is but a refraction of his rough-and- tumble self. Sandburg died at the ripe old age of 89. Like Ulysses of old, he was a man of twists and turns who had drunk the rich varietals of this world to the lees.

William Wordsworth (1770-1850)

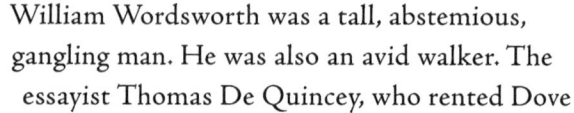

William Wordsworth was a tall, abstemious, gangling man. He was also an avid walker. The essayist Thomas De Quincey, who rented Dove Cottage in the Lake District after Wordsworth and his growing family moved on, minces no words about it:

> His legs were pointedly condemned by all female connoisseurs in legs; not that they were bad in any way which would force itself upon your notice—there was no absolute deformity about them; and undoubtedly they had been serviceable legs beyond the average standard of human requisition; for I calculate, upon good data, that with these identical legs Wordsworth must have traversed a distance of 175,000 to 180,000 English

miles—a mode of exertion which, to him, stood in the stead of alcohol and other stimulants whatsoever to animal spirits; to which, indeed, he was indebted for a life of unclouded happiness, and we for much of what is most excellent in his writings.
(*Literary and Lake Reminiscences*)

The phrase we excerpt on page 31 comes from the opening stich of what is perhaps the best-known of hundreds of poems Wordsworth conceived upon a ramble.

> I wandered lonely as a cloud
> That floats on high o'er vales and hills,
> When all at once I saw a crowd,
> A host, of golden daffodils;
> Beside the lake, beneath the trees,
> Fluttering and dancing in the breeze.

A poem, Wordsworth declares in his manifesto, the Preface to *Lyrical Ballads* (1798), "takes its origin from emotion recollected in tranquility." In other words, you go for a walk, feel awed by Nature's beauty, give it all a think, then write a crisp poem about it when you get home. This is exactly the M.O. at work here, as is signaled in the poem's final stanza:

> For oft, when on my couch I lie
> In vacant or in pensive mood,

> They flash upon that inward eye
> Which is the bliss of solitude;
> And then my heart with pleasure fills,
> And dances with the daffodils.

Lyrical Ballads was a joint project Wordsworth produced with his friend and fellow poet Samuel Taylor Coleridge. Their collection, we now see with the benefit of hindsight, inaugurated the so-called Romantic period in English letters. It is often thought that Coleridge, arguably the more learned of the two, exerted the greatest intellectual influence on Wordsworth. But Wordsworth's peripatetic aesthetic springs from another source entirely. While a young man visiting Revolutionary Paris in 1792, Wordsworth met the eccentric John Stewart (1747–1822), nicknamed "Walking" Stewart, owing to the fact that over the course of thirty years he had made his way on foot from Madras, India (where he had worked as a clerk for the East India Company) through Persia, Arabia, Abyssinia, North Africa, and Europe, reaching as far East as St. Petersburg, and as far West as North America, before settling for a spell in Paris, and, later, London. Walking Stewart seems to have fallen in with some Indian sages while working out East because he concocted an eclectic philosophy of Nature that combined Epicurean atomism and Heraclitean flux with the "no-self" doctrine of Buddhism and the intriguing idea that "all composition is decomposition." He expounded this gospel in at least thirty books, including the verse treatise of 1791 *The Apocalypse of Nature*. An obituary with the stupendous title *The Life and Adventures of the Celebrated Walking Stewart, Including his Travels in the East Indies, Turkey, Germany,*

& America, by a Relative, with a Portrait (London, 1822) recounts another of Stewart's teachings that seems also to have left its mark on an impressionable young Wordsworth:

> Mr. Stewart used to observe that the deplorable effect of too much book learning is to deprive man of self-examination, through an overstuffed memory, which prevents the exercise of the faculties of imagination ... and to make conscience depend on the will of others, and not on self-knowledge.

Compare with this sentiment these stanzas from Wordsworth's poem (from *Lyrical Ballads*) "The Tables Turned":

> One impulse from a vernal wood
> May teach you more of man,
> Of moral evil and of good,
> Than all the sages can.
>
> Sweet is the lore which Nature brings;
> Our meddling intellect
> Mis-shapes the beauteous forms of things:—
> We murder to dissect.

Vachel Lindsay (1879-1931)

Vachel Lindsay is America's true-blue hobo poet. Born in Springfield, Illinois, young Vachel set off on various paths, first as a medical student at Hiram College in Ohio, then studying painting at the Art Institute of Chicago and The New York School of Art (now The New School) before finding his calling as a poetic carnival barker plying an art form that he called "The Higher Vaudeville." Others dubbed him, somewhat more charitably, "The Prairie Troubabor," as Lindsay traveled all over the country declaiming and even singing his works. Lindsay's poetry puts a premium on performance and on sound—its pulsing succession of consonants and vowels, rhythm and beat—as in his best-known poem, "The Congo":

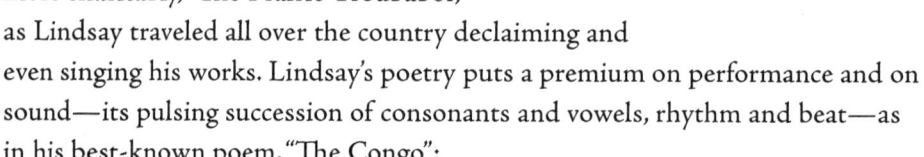

> A roaring, epic, rag-time tune
> From the mouth of the Congo
> To the Mountains of the Moon.
> Death is an Elephant,
> Torch-eyed and horrible,
> Foam-flanked and terrible.
> BOOM, steal the pygmies,

> BOOM, kill the Arabs,
> BOOM, kill the white men,
> HOO, HOO, HOO.

Lindsay's canticles and raps are sprinkled with dramatic notations like "with a philosophic pause," or "shrilly, and with a heavily accented metre."

Enter Charles Ives (1874-1954). Ives was an insurance executive from Connecticut whose first love was composing music that makes Arnold Schoenberg sound like Tin Pan Alley. On page 32 T. Motley cleverly superimposes a phrase from Lindsay's "General William Booth Enters into Heaven" onto the score of Ives's setting of that poem. Its titular character, the larger-than-life William Booth, founded the charitable organization The Salvation Army. Ives was an urbane sophisticate who had a soft spot for Americana, hence the musical setting. Lindsay, on the other hand, was a staunch, passionate advocate for social and racial justice. "Booth led boldly with his big bass drum" continues in this vein:

> Walking lepers followed, rank on rank,
> Lurching bravoes from the ditches dank,
> Drabs from the alleyways and drug fiends pale—
> Minds still passion-ridden, soul-powers frail:—
> Vermin-eaten saints with mouldy breath,
> Unwashed legions with the ways of Death—

In the end, alas, the world's decrepitude and his own financial troubles got the worse of Lindsay's better angels: He took his own life by drinking a bottle of lye in 1931, at the height of a Great Depression.

John Donne (1572-1631)

John Donne eloped to marry for love. He became a priest. And he wrote some very clever poems about sex. Mind you, he did not do all these things in that order, but his swashbuckling life is one of the most eventful of the period. Indeed, to look at the portrait of him as a young man hanging in London's National Gallery, you'd think he was a pirate. Donne, in fact, *was* a soldier of fortune in his early years. He was also a Catholic, which did him no favors in Tudor England. Worse still, he married Anne More without her stately father's permission, which cost him his job and got him thrown into prison. Donne's penchant for poetic puns, however, was apparent even then, under duress, when, according to his earliest biographer, he signed a prison letter to his new bride explaining his sudden predicament: "John Donne, Anne Donne, Undone." Twelve children later, his beloved Anne dead herself delivering the last of the litter (a stillborn), Donne the Catholic took orders as a priest in the Church of England and later became Dean of St. Paul's Cathedral. The line on page 33 ("Death, Be Not Proud") comes from this period (*Holy Sonnets* No. 10), but it is not necessarily Donne's best or last word on the topic. In Meditation No. 17 from *Devotions upon Emergent Occasions* (1624), written while he was feverish and on his death bed (or so he thought), Donne penned perhaps his most famous lines:

> No man is an Iland, intire of itselfe; every man
> is a peece of the Continent, a part of the maine;
> if a Clod bee washed away by the Sea, Europe
> is the lesse, as well as if a Promontorie were, as
> well as if a Manor of thy friends or of thine
> owne were; any mans death diminishes me,
> because I am involved in Mankinde;
> And therefore never send to know for whom
> the bell tolls; It tolls for thee.

And then there's the erotica. Consider this for a come on, from a poem of Donne's early days entitled "The Flea":

> Mark but this flea, and mark in this,
> How little that which thou deniest me is;
> It sucked me first, and now sucks thee,
> And in this flea our two bloods mingled be;
> Thou know'st that this cannot be said
> A sin, nor shame, nor loss of maidenhead,
> Yet this enjoys before it woo,

>   And pampered swells with one blood made of two,
>   And this, alas, is more than we would do.

That the letters "s" and "f" looked identical in English typeface in Donne's time I leave to the imagination of the reader.

Alfred, Lord Tennyson (1809-1892)

With a pompous name like that, you'd think Tennyson was a born aristocrat. He certainly wouldn't be the first poet who was. Lord Byron, for example, was a real Lord. But Tennyson wasn't. It was only years later, after he replaced Wordsworth as Poet Laureate of Great Britain and Ireland in 1850, that Gladstone, the Prime Minister, offered him the baronetcy that inducted him into the House of Lords. (And he had twice refused the honor.) Rather, as a young man Tennyson had to quit college without getting a degree to go home and support his mother and nine siblings after his father had died. Soon thereafter his best friend also died, who had been engaged to marry his sister. Some of Tennyson's best poems are meditations on this loss and concomitant despair, including the memorable "Ulysses" from 1833. "Ring Out, Wild Bells," whose leading line appears on page 34, is measuredly happier. Published the year Tennyson was appointed Laureate, the poem was supposedly composed on New Year's Eve and contains the line, now a popular phrase, "Ring out the old, ring in the new." Tennyson is a sentimental, patriotic poet. But sentimentality and patriotism of this sort rings true for our time, too:

> Ring out a slowly dying cause,
> And ancient forms of party strife;
> Ring in the nobler modes of life,
> With sweeter manners, purer laws.

T. S. Eliot (1888-1965)

Thomas Stearns Eliot wrote the book of whimsical poems that later became the musical *Cats*, a Broadway blockbuster subsequently made into a film that you'll want to be sure to miss. That's hard to believe, because Eliot was highbrow, and seemed to take himself quite seriously. He was born in St. Louis, Missouri, but, an Anglophile at heart, he moved to the UK to study at Oxford in his twenties (after earning degrees from Harvard), and became a British citizen. His marriage to Vivienne Haigh-Wood, a hypochondriac and/

or psychopath depending on how charitable a view one takes, contributed to considerable unhappiness in Eliot's prime of life and provided ample fodder for a rather different film, *Tom and Viv* (1994), which is, for the record, much better than *Cats*. In any event, it was in the despondent frame of mind arising from an unhappy marriage that Eliot wrote his masterpieces "The Waste Land" (1922) and "The Hollow Men" (1925), from which we invert a phrase on page 36:

> This is the way the world ends
> This is the way the world ends
> This is the way the world ends
> Not with a bang but a whimper.

The Ring-around-the-Rosie repetition of these lines, the poem's last, reflects the existential angst and ennui of early Modernism. ("Ashes, ashes, we all fall down!" is how the traditional jingle Eliot alludes to here concludes in the American version.) Page 44 quotes the opening lines of another well-known T. S. poem, "The Love Song of J. Alfred Prufrock" (1915), which we pair with a phrase from Robert Frost (more on whom below). In the original, Eliot compares the evening that beckons, "spread out against the sky," to a "patient etherized upon a table." The journey of this wayfaring traveler, it is implied, will be by way of astral projection, through a visionary landscape of the mind. Indeed, "Prufrock" is prefaced by Eliot, revealingly, by lines quoted in Italian from Dante's *Inferno*, where an inhabitant of the Eighth Circle of Hell warns the poet, and through him us, that as a species we may have reached the point of no return: ***giammai di questo fondo / non tornò vivo alcun.*** "Up from these depths, no one has yet returned alive." Whether it'll be a whimper or a bang, I suppose we all shall see soon enough.

William Blake (1757-1827)

William Blake was producing illustrated poems long before anyone ever uttered the words "graphic novel" or "comic book." Almost all of his published work is hand-lettered and incorporates pictures. These take the form of watercolors, etchings, and engravings in a unique style that melds classicism and fantasy. Before Blake, Hellenistic poets dabbled in so-called concrete poetry, e.g., poems written down in the shape of an egg, an axe, a set of Pan pipes, etc., and the monks who produced medieval manuscripts often drew figural and decorated letters called historiated initials at the beginning of chapters or paragraphs. Blake, however, took the interaction of word and image to another level. In many ways the poetic art of this book is an homage to his genius. Pages 37-39 reproduce the first lines of *Auguries of Innocence* (1803). The poem consists of a series of scenarios, expressed in rhyming couplets, wherein human wrongdoing portends some larger impending doom. Most interesting for our age perhaps are the warnings attached to the mistreatment of Nature's non-human agents:

A Robin Red breast in a Cage
Puts all Heaven in a Rage

A dog starvd at his Masters Gate
Predicts the ruin of the State

Each outcry of the hunted Hare
A fibre from the Brain does tear

He who shall hurt the little Wren
Shall never be belovd by Men

Kill not the Moth nor Butterfly
For the Last Judgment draweth nigh

For every action, it is implied, there is an equal and opposite reaction. Ironically, one of Blake's masterworks is a painting of Isaac Newton as an evil demiurge. Blake dismissed Newton's universal Laws (of which the formulation above is the Third, of Motion) as hubristic and mechanistic. ("Art is the Tree of Life. Science is the Tree of Death" is Blake's blunt verdict on that topic.) And yet the *Auguries* underscore in more oblique idiom essentially the same point, namely the extent to which everything is connected, and that no one in this world can act with impunity.

John Milton (1608-1674)

By the time John Milton published his biblical epic, *Paradise Lost*, in 1664—one of the strangest, most visionary works the English language has ever produced—he had been totally blind for over ten years. Poetic blindness is an old mythological trope. The Thracian minstrel Thamyris, for example, was blinded by the Muses for daring to compete with them in song. But there's also Tiresias, the sage from Thebes, who for his blindness possessed second sight as a prophetic seer. Deprivation of one sense organ, the thinking has it, sharpens another. Such was the case with Homer, the traditionally blind bard whose *Iliad* and *Odyssey* are masterworks of oral-poetic artistry. Lest you think it only a trope, however, consider Miihkali Perttunen, the blind, illiterate peasant from Karelia who in the mid-nineteenth century recited over 3,500 lines of pagan rune song to Elias Lönnrot, a country doctor and amateur folklorist, for a collection that later became the sprawling *Kalevala*, Finland's national epic. And it's not just illiterate peasants or mythological figures. Jorge Luis Borges is a twentieth-century Tiresias, just as James Joyce (only half-blind) is a modern Homer. Borges' verbal labyrinths spin out tapestries for the inner eye that take considerable second sight to see, while Joyce's poetic prose is nothing if not music to the ear.

The lines excerpted on page 41 are the final lines of a sonnet that Milton composed shortly after he himself went blind (No. 19, "When I consider how my light is spent"). Scholars think it may have been dictated to his friend and fellow *POEM* quipster Andrew Marvell (see *infra*). "They also serve who only stand and wait" is not only Milton's abjuration of self-pity, it is also a validation of the *vita contemplativa* over against the *vita activa* that characterized educated men of his revolutionary age—an age that saw Oliver Cromwell top King Charles I in the English Civil War. *Paradise Lost,* from which we lift a phrase on page 40, was dictated by Milton to his daughters. Reports suggest it was not a pleasant experience for either party. Old men lacking sight or sound can be— stereotypically, perhaps—grumpy and tyrannical. Fortunately (and also perhaps stereotypically) poets often leverage emotional dissonance into a creative tension that produces works of unusual power. In Milton's case which it was will be in the eye, as it were, of the beholder.

Elizabeth Barrett Browning (1806-1861)

Elizabeth Barrett was the Victorian Sappho. Not that she was a lesbian, so far as we know. And not that Sappho herself necessarily was either, in any strict sense, as she was married, and had a daughter. Barrett's own passionate, yet equally Platonic, courtship and later marriage to fellow poet Robert Browning suggests she herself was quite straight. But, like Sappho, Barrett rivaled her male peers in terms of poetic quality, output, and popularity. (She was short-listed for Poet

Laureate the year Tennyson got it.) Also like Sappho, but unlike some female contemporaries—the Brontë sisters, for example—she always published under her own name, not the made-up *nom de plume* of a man. Barrett was sickly from a young age, suffering from a spinal condition and TB. She took *laudanum* to dull the pain, whose agonies and ecstasies are ably recounted by Thomas De Quincey in ***Confessions of an English Opium Eater*** (1821). Perhaps the *laudanum* is what made her a fierce Christian mystic who believed that "Christ's religion is essentially poetry—poetry glorified." But Barrett was not a fanatic, nor a dissolute. She was studious, multi-lingual (conversant in both ancient Greek and Hebrew), and a prolific letter writer. A language she did not know, however, was Portuguese—this in spite of the fact that the collection from which a phrase on page 42 is lifted is entitled ***Sonnets from the Portuguese*** (1845). "How do I love thee?" Barrett asks. "Let me count the ways." The book's title was a privacy ruse to make the reader think the intimate love poems it contained were translations from some other person, from some other place and time. Here is the whole of that sonnet (No. 43), unadulterated:

> How do I love thee? Let me count the ways.
> I love thee to the depth and breadth and height
> My soul can reach, when feeling out of sight
> For the ends of being and ideal grace.
> I love thee to the level of every day's
> Most quiet need, by sun and candle-light.
> I love thee freely, as men strive for right.
> I love thee purely, as they turn from praise.

I love thee with the passion put to use
In my old griefs, and with my childhood's faith.
I love thee with a love I seemed to lose
With my lost saints. I love thee with the breath,
Smiles, tears, of all my life; and, if God choose,
I shall but love thee better after death.

Gaius Valerius Catullus (84-54 BCE)

Catullus was proficient at the short, piquant poem.

Odi et amo. Quare id faciam fortasse requires?
Nescio, sed fieri sentio et excrucior.

"I hate and I love. Why do I do it, perhaps you will ask? / I have no idea, but I feel it happening and it's like being crucified!" This terse elegiac couplet, to which we allude on page 43, reads like stenographic shorthand for the whole poetic impulse. A poem is a pinch on the arm or, sometimes, a kick in the arse to check that we're still alive. The source of Catullus's reveries and torment was his mistress, Clodia, an older married woman of the august Metelli family. She was also his muse, whom he nicknamed "Lesbia" after the Greek poet Sappho. Catullus's hallmark poem to Clodia is No. 5 in the "little book" (*libellus*) that he dedicated to Cornelius Nepos:

Vivamus, mea Lesbia, atque amemus,
rumoresque senum severiorum
omnes unius aestimemus assis!
soles occidere et redire possunt;
nobis, cum semel occidit brevis lux,
nox est perpetua una dormienda.
da mi basia mille, deinde centum,
dein mille altera, dein secunda centum,
deinde usque altera mille, deinde centum;
dein, cum milia multa fecerimus,
conturbabimus illa, ne sciamus,
aut ne quis malus invidere possit,
cum tantum sciat esse basiorum.

Let us live, my Lesbia, but let's also love,
and deem all gossip from dour
old men as worth one pence.
Suns can die and rise again,
but we, once our brief light's spent,
must sleep on through one endless night.
So: Give me a thousand kisses;
then a hundred; then a thousand more;
then a second hundred; then,
once we have done it many thousand times,

> we'll muddle them up, so we no longer know
> how many kisses there were,
> and no wanker can begrudge them us.

But Catullus is about more than kisses. Ezra Pound once opined "You read Catullus to prevent yourself from being poisoned by the lies of pundits . . . to purge yourself of the greasy sediments of lecture courses." Fellow poet Robert Graves brought Catullus with him to the trenches of WWI. T. E. Lawrence is said to have carried the poems of Catullus in his saddlebags as he fomented revolt in the sands of Arabia. Another smart adventurer, Sir Walter Raleigh, translated some of the first bit of Poem No. 5 as an epigraph to his *Historie of the World* (1677). Sir Walter wrote that tome, shackled for treason, in the Tower of London.

> The Sunne may set and rise
> But we contrariwise
> Sleepe after our short light
> One everlasting night.

Catullus was a debutant among the avant-garde of late Republican Rome. He belongedto a group of poets that called themselves *Neoterics*, or the "Newer set." But his poeticsensibilities have outlived that fleeting, fashionable moment. They are perpetual, like the *nox* of No. 5.

Robert Frost (1874-1963)

Robert Frost was once my neighbor here in Vermont. By most accounts, no one liked him. He also lived in New Hampshire—a very different place from Vermont—where he was liked even less. Both states are north of Boston, the title of Frost's breakthrough collection of poems, published in 1914. Dead at 88, his iconic face seasoned and creased like a shriveled Macintosh, he had lived long enough to annoy many people. If Frost could be a curmudgeon in private, however, we should probably excuse him for it. His father died of TB when he was 11, leaving the family penniless; his mother of cancer when he was 26. Of the six children he had with his wife and high school sweetheart Elinor, one died of cholera, one of purpureal fever, and one by suicide. Another went insane. Only two children, daughters Lesley and Irma, outlived him. Elinor herself contracted breast cancer then died of heart failure in 1938. "About suffering they were never wrong," wrote Frost's contemporary, W. H. Auden, in the poem "Musée des Beaux Arts" (about Brueghel's painting *The Fall of Icarus*), *the Old Masters: how well they understood / Its human position: how it takes place / While someone else is eating or opening a window or just walking dully along.* In view of painful aspects and vistas it is sometimes best to say nothing and let a poet's poetry speak for itself. The pensive poem from which we excerpt a phrase on page 45 goes like this:

Two roads diverged in a yellow wood,
And sorry I could not travel both
And be one traveler, long I stood
And looked down one as far as I could
To where it bent in the undergrowth;

Then took the other, as just as fair,
And having perhaps the better claim,
Because it was grassy and wanted wear;T
hough as for that the passing there
Had worn them really about the same,

And both that morning equally lay
In leaves no step had trodden black.
Oh, I kept the first for another day!
Yet knowing how way leads on to way,
I doubted if I should ever come back.

I shall be telling this with a sigh
Somewhere ages and ages hence:
Two roads diverged in a wood, and I—
I took the one less traveled by,
And that has made all the difference.

William Shakespeare (1564-1616)

As far as William Shakespeare is concerned, to be or not to be—or, rather, *to have been*, or not—that is the question. Was the Elizabethan Bard of Avon, Master of Tragedy, Comedy, and Sonnet, actually Francis Bacon? Was he Christopher Marlowe? Or the Seventeenth Earl of Oxford? Scholars can protest too much on this topic, methinks, for if music be the food of love, and we live by food, leave the Bard alone and let him play on. What's in a name, anyhow? A rose by any other name would smell as sweet. In these matters the better part of valor is always discretion. Besides, all the *world's* a stage, and *all* the men and women merely players. They have their exits and entrances. One man in his time plays many parts . . . Sonnet XXIX, to which we allude on our final page, provides ample proof of Shakespeare's most constant themes, that all that glisters is not gold, and that all's well, that, well, *ends:*

> When, in disgrace with fortune and men's eyes,
> I all alone beweep my outcast state,
> And trouble deaf heaven with my bootless cries,
> And look upon myself and curse my fate,
> Wishing me like to one more rich in hope,

Featured like him, like him with friends possessed,
Desiring this man's art and that man's scope,
With what I most enjoy contented least;
Yet in these thoughts myself almost despising,
Haply I think on thee, and then my state,
Like to the lark at break of day arising
From sullen earth) sings hymns at heaven's gate;
   For thy sweet love remembered such wealth brings
   That then I scorn to change my state with kings.

M. D. Usher (1966-)

Einstein is reported to have said that the secret to creativity lies in knowing how to hide your sources. Usher, author of *POEM* and sundry lesser works, is deeply unoriginal in this sense, as he admits to stealing freely from the better ideas of others. He likes to invoke famous people and great works of art and literature because it makes him feel that what he aspires to is actually within his reach. Usher used to be an expert on centos, the art form employed in this book to plumb the depths of poetic technique and enjoyment. Now he occasionally composes them. He is a Classicist by training but makes his academic home in a department of Geography. He is also a farmer and a carpenter. He's a hack of all trades, really. Or a Protean figure, which sounds more mysterious. One big thing he knows is true is this, which is probably best expressed—how else?—with a poem. I expect he would consider it a dedication.

Ménage à trois

All that is
they call love
is not all

that we have.
Nothing is
more than this:

I am yours.
You are mine.
That is all.

T. Motley (1958-)

Comic artist and illustrator T. Motley is influenced by the formalist writers of the Oulipo group. His comics, many of which can be read at tmotley.com , feature panels nested within panels, paper-folding instructions, fourth wall breaks, and the like. He thinks of them as prototypes for directions the comic medium might grow.

He's happiest when he's teaching the

craft of cartooning to new generations, which he currently does online via the School of Visual Arts.

Publications and illustrated books over the years include *Cartozia Tales*, *The Brooklyn Rail*, Rikki Ducornet's "The One Marvelous Thing," and "The Golden Ass" by M. D. Usher.

FURTHER READING for *POEM*

The Princeton Encyclopedia of Poetry and Poetics, edited by Roland Greene, Stephen Cushman, *et al.* 4th edition (Princeton University Press, 2012)

Kenneth Koch, *Rose, Where Did You Get That Red? Teaching Great Poetry to Children* (Vintage, 1990; originally published by Random House, 1973)

Ted Hughes, *By Heart: 101 Poems to Remember*. Reprint edition. (Faber & Faber, 2000; originally published in 1997)

John Hollander, *Rhyme's Reason: A Guide to English Verse*. 4th edition. (Yale University Press, 2014)

Maureen McLane, *My Poets* (Farrar, Straus & Giroux, 2012)

Robert Graves, *The White Goddess: A Historical Grammar of Poetic Myth* (Farrar, Straus & Giroux, 2013; originally published in 1948)

Mary Oliver, *A Poetry Handbook: A Prose Guide to Writing and Understanding Poetry* (Mariner Books, 1994)

www.ingramcontent.com/pod-product-compliance
Lightning Source LLC
Chambersburg PA
CBHW041101070526
44579CB00003B/30